PU

Julie Brooke

Contents

Introduction

Shortbread is one of the simplest, yet most delicious, treats you can make. You can create a masterpiece with four basic ingredients: butter, sugar, flour and salt. Of course, shortbread is a lot more than that however. The recipes in this book offer a huge variety of shortbread in all its various forms from almond to chocolate drizzled, from lemon and lavender to rhubarb or vanilla rose and much, much more.

There is a long tradition of shortbread, starting from Scotland, but shortbread also lends itself to innovation and creation with both sweet and savory masterpieces. Inside these pages, you will find 50 recipes that will delight and intrigue everyone from those who have limited experience of the delights of shortbread to the seasoned expert.

I have always loved making shortbread and have found it to be incredibly popular with friends and family. It's a buttery, crumbly, crunchy delight that goes so well with various accompaniments, both sweet and savory. It can complement a lovely cup of hot tea or coffee just as well as a savory version fits with a cold glass of wine. It's a perfect all-rounder cookie or biscuit that suits every occasion and every palette. What's more, it's easy to make, does not require rare or exotic ingredients and delights both children and adults alike.

Read on now to discover how to make perfect shortbread, learn the top shortbread tips and bake the best 50 shortbread recipes you find anywhere, all in one collection!

Equipment

The following are important pieces of equipment that will prove invaluable when making your shortbread. You probably have all of them anyway, but it's worth going over a couple of details first.

The food processor or electric whisk

While in no way essential, a food processor will make life a little easier when making shortbread. Use it in quick pulses to mix your ingredients, creating a light and fluffy dough with not much effort and in far less time. If you don't have a full food processor, then an electric whisk will do the trick just as well.

If you do not have access to either a food processor or a whisk however, don't despair. You will just have a little more work to do manually. Consider it great exercise in preparation for the treat to come!

Wire Racks

The shortbread will need to cool before being served so a set of wire racks is essential. Some of the ingredients call for the shortbread to be drizzled with chocolate or other toppings. Ensure the shortbread has fully cooled before adding on the extra layer.

Baking sheet

I always use baking sheets as I prefer the slightly-raised edges on them which cookie sheets do not have. I tend to opt for the heavier sheets as I find they last longer and are much better at distributing the heat evenly across the entire sheet which makes baking uniform cookies easier. They also warp less in the heat and the washing-up afterwards.

Lighter colored sheets will not retain heat for as long as darkly-colored sheets which will affect how your shortbread appears after baking. If you find the bottoms of the shortbread are too dark, then adjust the oven down slightly to compensate.

I use parchment paper for all my shortbread recipes, in which case you don't need to worry about the sheet being non-stick or not. This means you don't need to buy the more expensive variety and saves on the washing-up later as well. It's most likely you already have your favorite baking sheets at home already. There is no need to buy anything new – sticking to what you know usually produces the best results.

Rolling pin

Needed for some recipes to roll out the dough to the required thickness. A heavy, tapered rolling pin is a joy to use and should last many years.

Large Bowl

You will need to mix a lot of ingredients and after seeing how popular your shortbread is, you might want to double the recipe from time to time. A large mixing bowl is essential.

Sharp knife

You will need a knife for some recipes to cut the dough into the right shapes before adding to the oven. Your favorite knife will be fine here.

Cookie cutters

Again, your favorite cookie cutters are perfect. You can cut the dough into whatever shape you prefer from the traditional to the more adventurous.

Parchment Paper

Used on the baking sheets to prevent sticking and residue remaining on your baking sheets. There is no need to add anything else to the parchment paper. Just press it down onto the baking sheet and add your dough.

Plastic Wrap

It's critical you chill the dough in the fridge first before you add it to the oven. Wrap it in plastic wrap first and chill for at least an hour.

Ingredients

One of the things that makes shortbread so simple to make is the small number of ingredients that you require. As there are not many ingredients for each recipe, I normally recommend getting the highest quality ingredients you can for your shortbread as the difference can be significant. Here are a few points about specific items.

Butter – assume when the recipes talk about butter, that it is unsalted.

Flour – All-purpose flour is used in all recipes unless stated otherwise.

Sugar – For most of the recipes in this book where sugar is mentioned, it should be assumed that it is white sugar. Where it is not, I have stated otherwise e.g. brown sugar or confectioners' as well. White sugar will lend a little more crunch to your shortbread while a brown sugar will give it a little more of a caramel flavor.

Salt – where salt is mentioned as part of the dough, table salt is fine. Where used as part of a topping, on chocolate for example, the larger-flaked sea salt is best.

Vanilla – almost all these recipes call for vanilla extract. I love vanilla and always have to hold myself back from adding too much, but it does go beautifully with shortbread.

Chocolate Chips – in most of the recipes here these are mini chocolate chips and semi-sweet. Feel free to adapt to dark chocolate or white if you prefer.

Top 8 Shortbread Making Tips

The following tips are all made so you can make the very best shortbread in the easiest and quickest way possible. They come from several years of making these recipes and should help you get an immediate head start to create some wonderful shortbread masterpieces.

1.) Once you have made the dough, it is vital that you chill it afterwards before the bake. If you are going to cut the dough into rounds, I recommend rolling the dough into a log shape and covering in plastic wrap before adding it the fridge for at least an hour. Two hours or overnight even is fine. If you are going to roll the dough out on a surface and use cookie cutters, then the shape is less important.

2.) You may need to experiment a little with the baking time. Not only will this vary from oven to oven, but the amount of time also determines how soft or hard the shortbread will be. The less time in the oven the softer and slightly chewier it becomes. The more time, the harder and crunchier it will be. The recipes in this book assume that the oven has been pre-heated to 350F. The times given produce a middle ground between soft and hard which you can then alter yourself depending on your own preference.

3.) Timing is important. Keep an eye on your shortbread biscuits, especially the first few times once they have entered the oven. They should be a pale gold color, without going brown or burnt on the bottoms.

4.) Don't overmix your dough. It can be easy to get carried away, especially with kitchen equipment that takes away the manual labor element and overmix your dough. You should mix enough until all the ingredients have just combined. If you are mixing by hand and it is proving hard work, you can try grating in chilled butter.

5.) There are not many ingredients to shortbread, so I always recommend getting the best quality flour, sugar and butter you can find. They are the core ingredients to the dish and a little extra quality here will be noticeable.

6.) Experiment and be brave! If you like your shortbread a little sweeter, then try some more sugar. If you like a strong vanilla taste, then try another teaspoon. If you think it would work well with a different fruit or nut or a little more chocolate, then do give it a try. Remember that while shortbread is often regarded as a sweet treat, it doesn't have to be. I have included some savory recipes in this book as well which will provide fabulous hors d'oeuvres for any party. Shortbread goes well with cheese for example or a savory jam. It really does suit any occasion.

7.) Don't be afraid to play around with the shape of your shortbread either. Traditionally it comes in three forms. It can be made in a large circular shape which is then cut into slices or a rectangle-like shape or many smaller circles. Try all three to see which you prefer and use your own cookie cutters to experiment with different sizes and thickness.

8.) Shortbread will last a long time when stored correctly. Keep it in a sealed container in a cool location. Shortbread will freeze, but you are better off freezing the uncooked dough and baking it when required.

I very much hope you will enjoy all the different shortbread recipes in this book. They have proved immensely popular with friends and family over decades and I am so pleased and honored to have the opportunity to share them with you now. Without further delay – bring on the recipes and happy baking!

Free Gift

I would love to send you an entirely free gift – my Top 100 Cupcake Recipes. This is a whole book dedicated to the wonderful world of cupcakes and contains 100 fantastic, easy to make recipes. If you would like to get a free copy, then just follow the link below and I'll get it out to you straightaway!

Just visit here - http://eepurl.com/bWd-XL - for a free copy of the Top 100 Cupcake Recipes!

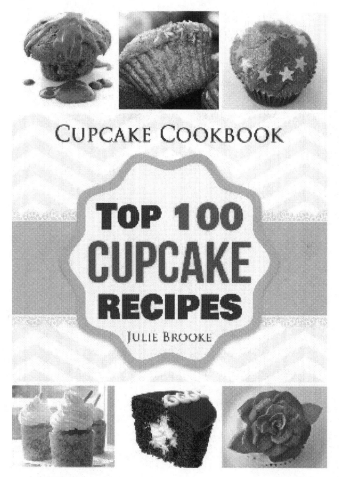

Almond Shortbread

Everything gets better with chocolate and marshmallows. It gets better still with the addition of shortbread. Try these for a popular, sweet treat.

Ingredients

2 cups all purpose flour

1 cup butter

½ cup sugar

½ teaspoon salt

1 teaspoon vanilla

2 teaspoons almond extract

½ cup almonds, chopped

30 whole almonds

1 tablespoon confectioners' sugar

Instructions

Preheat oven to 350F. Add the butter, vanilla, almond extract and sugar together and mix until fluffy. Add in the flour and salt, followed by the almonds and mix again. Divide the dough into 2 log shapes, cover in plastic wrap and add to the fridge for at least an hour.

Remove from the fridge and cut into ¼ inch thick rounds. Place on a baking tray. You can add an almond onto each cookie by pressing lightly down on the dough. Bake for about 15 minutes or until golden. Remove to cool on a wire rack. Add a light dusting of confectioners' sugar and serve.

Apple Shortbread Slices

I think these work beautifully as they are, but I have friends who make these with an extra cup of mini chocolate chips. Try both and see which you prefer.

Ingredients

2 cup all purpose flour

1 ½ cups butter

½ cup sugar, white

½ cup sugar brown

2 teaspoons vanilla

½ teaspoon salt

2 cups apples, peeled and thinly sliced

1 teaspoon cinnamon

1 teaspoon nutmeg

Instructions

Preheat oven to 350F. Add the butter, white sugar and vanilla together and mix until fluffy. Add in the flour and salt and mix until just combined. Add 2/3 of the mixture to a pre-prepared 9x13 inch pan. Bake for about 20 minutes or until golden and remove from the oven.

In another pan, add the apples, brown sugar, cinnamon and nutmeg together. Spread the apple mixture evenly around the shortbread crust. Add the remainder of the dough and place back in the oven for a further 20 minutes.

Remove from the oven and leave to sit for 5 minutes before placing on a wire rack to cool. Cut into squares and serve.

Apricot Shortbread

Ingredients

2 cups all purpose flour

1 cup butter

½ cup sugar

1 teaspoon vanilla

½ teaspoon salt

1 cup dried apricots, chopped

Instructions

Preheat oven to 350F. Add the butter, vanilla and sugar into a bowl and mix until fluffy. Add in the flour and salt and sit again. Fold in the apricots. Remove the dough, fashion it into two equal sized log shapes and cover in plastic wrap. Add to the fridge for at least an hour.

Remove from the fridge and cut into ¼ inch thick rounds. Place on a pre-prepared baking sheet and bake for about 12 to 14 minutes or until golden. Remove to a wire rack to cool and serve.

Banana Nut Shortbread

If you dislike seeing browning bananas lingering sadly in the fruit bowl, then this is a great way to use them up to create a delicious shortbread. I like to add the nuts in at the end, however, it works well without them as well. If you like it a little sweeter, than you can also add a half cup of chocolate chips into the mix.

Ingredients

2 cups all purpose flour

1 cup butter, unsalted

½ teaspoon salt

½ cup sugar

1 teaspoon vanilla

3 bananas, mashed

½ teaspoon cinnamon

½ cup nuts, whole (pecan or walnuts go well)

Instructions

Preheat oven to 350F. Add the butter, sugar and vanilla into a bowl and mix until fluffy. Gradually add in the flour and salt and mix until just combined. Fold in the mashed bananas. Add the dough into a greased 10x10 inch pan and press down the nuts into the dough. Bake for about 30 minutes or until it has gone golden. Remove from the oven and let it cool in the pan for about 15 minutes. Remove to a wire rack to cool, cut and serve.

Blackberry Shortbread

Ingredients

2 cup all purpose flour

1 ½ cups butter

½ cup sugar

2 teaspoons vanilla

½ teaspoon salt

1 cup blackberry jam

1 tablespoon confectioners' sugar

Instructions

Preheat oven to 350F. Add the butter, vanilla and sugar together and mix until fluffy. Add the flour and salt and mix again until just combined. Divide the dough into two. Cover one half in plastic wrap and add to the fridge to cool for at least an hour. Add the remainder of the dough into a pre-prepared 9x9 inch pan. Press down lightly with your fingers so it compresses.

Add the pan to the oven and bake for about 20 minutes or until it becomes golden. Remove from the oven and allow to cool for a few minutes. Add the jam evenly around everywhere. Now add the remainder of the dough on top of the jam, crumbling it with your fingers as you do so. Place the pan back into the oven and bake for another 20 minutes or until golden again. Remove from the oven and let it sit for 5 minutes before placing on a wire rack to cool. Sprinkle with sugar, cut into the desired size and serve.

Blue Cheese and Rosemary Shortbread

Cheese is a favorite ingredient of mine and I try to get it into as many recipes as it fits. A strong blue cheese works perfectly here, offset by the fragrant rosemary, making them a perfect savory shortbread.

Ingredients

2 cups all purpose flour

1 cup butter

½ cup sugar

½ teaspoon salt

¼ teaspoon pepper

1 cup blue cheese

2 tablespoons rosemary, chopped

Instructions

Preheat oven to 350F. Add the butter and sugar and crumbled blue cheese together and mix until fluffy. Add the flour, salt and pepper in and mix until just combined. Remove the dough and separate into two even sized log shapes. Cover in plastic wrap and add to the fridge for at least an hour.

Once removed, cut the log into ¼ inch rounds and place on a pre-prepared baking tray. Add to the oven and bake for about 13-14 minutes or until golden. Remove from the oven to a wire rack to cool and serve with a refreshing glass of something cold.

Cardamom Shortbread

I like cardamom in either sweet or savory foods, but I feel it works particularly well with this shortbread recipe. You can get a lovely, light fragrant taste that is perfect for the summer months or the festive season.

Ingredients

2 cups all purpose flour

1 cup butter

½ cup sugar

½ teaspoon salt

2 teaspoons cardamom, ground

Instructions

Preheat oven to 350F. Add together the butter and sugar and mix until fluffy. Add in the salt, cardamom and flour until everything just comes together. Remove the dough and fashion into a ball. Cover in plastic wrap and add to the fridge for an hour.

Remove from the fridge and add to a floured surface. Roll out the dough to about ¼ inch thickness. Cut the dough into your preferred shape with a cookie cutter. Add the cookies to a baking tray and add to the oven for about 14 minutes or until golden. Remove to a wire rack to cool and serve.

Carrot Cake Shortbread

Carrot cake is an all-time favorite in our home, so finding a way to combine it with shortbread seemed a great idea. These are delicious and will not last long in your household – and they're full to the brim with carrots. I rarely add a frosting to shortbread, but it goes so well when doing a carrot cake and it works perfectly here as well.

Ingredients

2 cups all purpose flour

1 cup butter

½ teaspoon salt

½ cup carrots, grated

½ cup raisins

1 cup sugar, brown

1 teaspoon vanilla

2 teaspoons cinnamon

Frosting

1 package cream cheese, 8 ounces

1 cup confectioners' sugar

½ cup butter

½ teaspoon vanilla

Instructions

Preheat oven to 350F. Add the butter, vanilla and sugar together and mix until fluffy. Gradually add in the flour, salt and cinnamon until just combined. Finally, add the carrot and raisins and combine. Divide the mixture into two log shapes, cover in plastic wrap and add to the fridge for an hour.

Remove from the fridge and cut into ¼ inch thick rounds. Add to a baking tray and bake for 15 minutes or until golden. While they are baking, prepare the cream cheese frosting by adding the cream cheese, butter, sugar and vanilla together and mix until fully combined. Remove the shortbread once baked and remove to a wire rack to cool. Gently pipe over the frosting and serve!

Cheddar Shortbread

These are so good they will be gone in seconds at any party or gathering. I normally use cheddar as my cheese of choice but almost any flavor works well. The poppy seeds scattered throughout look amazing and add to the balance of the cookie that is guaranteed to prove a hit.

Ingredients

2 cups all purpose flour

1 cup butter, unsalted

½ teaspoon salt

1 cup cheddar cheese, grated

2 tablespoons poppy seeds

Instructions

Preheat oven to 350F. Add the flour, butter and salt together and mix. Fold in the cheese and poppy seeds. Divide the dough into two equal sized log shapes and cover in plastic wrap. Add to the fridge for at least an hour.

Remove from the fridge and cut into ¼ inch rounds. Add the rounds onto a baking tray and bake for about 15 minutes or until golden. Remove to a wire rack to cool and serve.

Chocolate and Chilli Shortbread

These add a little kick to the more traditional recipe, but the overall effect is delicious. You can vary the amount of chilli powder of course for your own taste.

Ingredients

2 cups all purpose flour

1 cup butter

½ cup sugar

½ teaspoon salt

1/3 cup cocoa

1 teaspoon vanilla

½ teaspoon cinnamon

½ teaspoon chilli powder

Instructions

Preheat oven to 350F. Add together the sugar, vanilla and butter into a bowl and mix until fluffy. Add in the flour, cocoa powder, salt, cinnamon and chilli powder and mix again. Remove and separate the dough into two equal sized log shapes. Cover in plastic wrap and add to the fridge for at least an hour.

Remove from the fridge and cut into ¼ inch thick rounds. Add them to a baking tray and bake for about 12 minutes. Remove and place on a wire rack to cool and serve.

Chocolate Cherry Shortbread

Ingredients

2 cups all purpose flour

1 cup butter, unsalted

1 teaspoon salt

½ cup sugar

1 teaspoon vanilla

½ teaspoon almond

1 cup maraschino cherries, chopped

½ cup mini chocolate chips

Instructions

Preheat oven to 350F. Drain the cherries and ensure they are dried and chopped into small pieces. Add the butter, sugar, vanilla and almond extracts into a bowl and mix until fluffy. Gradually add in the flour and sugar until just combined. Gently fold in the cherries and chocolate chips.

Divide the dough equally into two log shapes and cover in plastic wrap. Add them to the fridge for at least an hour. Once chilled, remove from the fridge and cut into ¼ inch rounds. Add to a baking sheet and bake for about 15 minutes or until golden. Remove to a wire rack to cool and serve.

Chocolate Chip Shortbread

Ingredients

2 cups all purpose flour

1 cup butter

½ cup sugar

½ teaspoon salt

1 cup chocolate chips

1 teaspoon vanilla

Instructions

Preheat oven to 350F. Add the flour and salt into a bowl and put to one side. In a separate bowl, add the butter, sugar and vanilla and cream together. Combine the flour bowl with the butter bowl, followed by the chocolate chips.

Using a spoon or ice-cream scoop, add balls of the mixture onto a baking sheet. Press down ever so slightly to give them a flatter surface. Bake for around 15 minutes or until golden. Remove from the oven, allow to cool slightly and serve warm or when completely cooled.

Chocolate Coconut Shortbread

Ingredients

2 cups all purpose flour

1 cup butter

½ cup sugar

1 teaspoon vanilla

½ teaspoon salt

1 cup coconut, shredded

1 cup chocolate chips, semisweet

Instructions

Preheat oven to 350F. Add the butter, vanilla and sugar into a bowl and mix until fluffy. Add in the salt and flour and mix again. Now add the shredded coconut and mix until everything has just come together. Fold in the chocolate chips.

Take a spoonful of dough and add it the baking tray. Press lightly down on each mound of dough to flatten them out and add to the oven. Bake for about 15 minutes or until golden. Remove and place on a wire rack to cool and then serve.

Chocolate Drizzled Butterscotch Shortbread

These might be a little indulgent, but they taste so good they're worth it every time!

Ingredients

2 cups all purpose flour

1 ½ cups butter

½ cup sugar, brown

1 teaspoon vanilla

½ teaspoon salt

1 cup butterscotch chips

½ cup chocolate chips, semisweet

Instructions

Preheat oven to 350F. Add the butter, vanilla and sugar together and mix until fluffy. Add in the flour and salt and mix until just combined. Fold in the butterscotch chips. Remove the dough and fashion into two log shapes. Cover in plastic wrap and add to the fridge for an hour.

Remove from the fridge and cut into rounds, about ¼ inch thick. Add to a pre-prepared baking sheet and bake for 12-14 minutes or until golden. Remove to a wire rack to cool. Melt the chocolate chips in the microwave or in a glass bowl over boiling water. Drizzle the melted chocolate over the shortbread. Allow the chocolate to harden and serve.

Cinnamon Shortbread

I've always loved the flavour of cinnamon in almost anything and shortbread of course is no exception. I normally have coffee with a cookie but try these with a steaming pot of tea for a lovely delicate taste every time. The perfect way to share a treat and catch-up with a friend!

Ingredients

2 cups all purpose flour

1 cup butter, unsalted

¾ cup sugar, brown

2 teaspoons cinnamon

½ teaspoon salt

Cinnamon Sugar

½ cup sugar

2 tablespoons cinnamon

Instructions

Preheat oven to 350F. Add the butter and sugar into a bowl and mix together. Add in the cinnamon, flour and salt into a bowl and sift together. Gradually add the flour bowl into the butter bowl and continue to mix in. Fashion the dough into a log shape and cover with plastic wrap. Add to the fridge for an hour.

Remove from the fridge and roll out the dough until it is about ¼ inch high. Cut out your cookies to the desired diameter and add to a prepared baking tray. Bake for about 15 minutes or until golden. Combine the sugar and cinnamon and sprinkle over the warm biscuits before serving.

Coconut and Lime Shortbread

These have a lovely spicy taste to them and go beautifully with a cup of tea. Popular at Christmas time of course, I enjoy having them throughout the year.

Ingredients

2 cups all purpose flour

1 cup butter, unsalted

½ cup sugar

½ teaspoon salt

1 teaspoon vanilla

½ cup coconut, shredded and toasted

Zest of 2 limes

Frosting

1 cup powdered sugar

½ teaspoon lime zest

½ tablespoon lime juice

Water

Instructions

Preheat oven to 350F. Add the sugar, lime zest, coconut and vanilla into a food processor and continue with pulses until everything is fine chopped. Add in the flour and repeat. Add in the butter lastly and repeat again. Remove from the food processor, cover in plastic wrap and add to the fridge for at least an hour.

Cut the dough into ¼ inch rounds and add to a baking tray. Bake for about 15 minutes or until golden. Remove to a wire rack to cool. Make the frosting by combining the powdered sugar, lime zest and lime juice. Add a little water if it becomes too thick or a little more sugar if too runny. Spoon over the biscuits with generous helpings and serve.

Cranberry Shortbread

Ingredients

2 cups all purpose flour

1 cup butter, unsalted

½ cup sugar

¼ teaspoon salt

½ cup cranberries, dried

1 teaspoon vanilla

½ teaspoon almond

1 tablespoons orange zest, grated

Instructions

Preheat over to 350F. Add the butter and sugar into a bowl and beat together until fluffy. Add in the almond and vanilla extract, followed by the orange zest. In a separate bowl, sift together the flour and the salt. Gradually add this to the butter bowl, continuing to mix as you do so. Add in the cranberries and mix again.

Separate the dough into two even sized log shapes and cover with plastic wrap. Place them in the fridge for at least an hour. Remove from the fridge and slice each log so each biscuit is around ¼ inch deep. Add to the oven for about 12 minutes until golden and remove to cool on a wire tray before serving.

Cream Cheese and Nut Shortbread

I've just used the more generic "nut" for these because they go so well with such a huge variety. I've tried pecans, walnuts, almonds and cashews and they've all turned out well. Try any of those or one of your own and you won't be disappointed.

Ingredients

2 cups all purpose flour

1 cup butter

4 ounces cream cheese

1 cup nuts, chopped

¾ cup sugar

1 teaspoon vanilla

1 teaspoon salt

Instructions

Preheat oven to 350F. Add the butter, cream cheese, vanilla and sugar into a bowl and mix until fluffy. Sift in the flour to another bowl, add the salt and then add to the butter bowl. Mix again until just combined and then fold in your nut of choice.

Remove the dough and fashion two equal sized logs. Cover in plastic wrap and add to the fridge for at least an hour. Remove and cut into rounds, ¼ inch thick. Add to a pre-prepared baking sheet and bake for about 15 minutes or until golden. Remove to a wire rack to cool and serve.

Double Chocolate Shortbread

Ingredients

2 cups all purpose flour

1 cup butter

½ cup sugar

½ cup cocoa powder

1 cup chocolate chips, semi-sweet

1 teaspoon vanilla

½ teaspoon salt

½ cup white chocolate chips

Instructions

Preheat oven to 350F. Add the butter, vanilla and sugar to a bowl and beat until fluffy. Add in the flour, cocoa powder and salt and mix again until everything is just combined. Fold in the chocolate chips. Divide the dough into two evenly sized log shapes, cover in plastic wrap and add to the fridge for at least an hour.

Remove from the fridge and cut into rounds of at least ¼ inch thick. Add to a pre-prepared baking sheet and bake for 13-15 minutes. Remove to a wire rack to cool completely. Melt the white chocolate chips in the microwave or in a glass bowl over boiling water. Drizzle over the cooled shortbread, wait for it to solidify and serve.

Double Quick Vanilla Shortbread

If speed is of the (vanilla) essence, then this recipe with five ingredients is the one for you. You can have these ready and on the table in under 30 minutes. They'll be eaten a lot quicker than that though.

Ingredients

2 cups all purpose flour

1 cup butter

½ cup sugar

2 teaspoons vanilla

½ teaspoon salt

Instructions

Preheat oven to 350F. Add the sugar, vanilla and butter together and mix until fluffy. Add in the flour and salt and mix again. Roll out the dough on to a floured surface to a little less than ½ inch thickness. Cut out the shapes with a cookie cutter and add to a baking tray. Bake for about 10-12 minutes or until golden.

Remove to a wire rack to cool and serve.

Fig, Maple and Walnut Shortbread

Ingredients

2 cups all purpose flour

1 cup butter

½ cup walnuts, chopped

¾ cup sugar

1 teaspoon vanilla

3 tablespoons maple syrup

½ cup figs, finely chopped

½ teaspoon salt

Instructions

Preheat oven to 350F. Add the butter, vanilla, maple syrup and sugar and mix until fluffy. Add in the flour, walnuts and salt and mix again. Fold in the figs. Separate the dough into two evenly sized logs, cover in plastic wrap and add to the fridge for at least an hour.

Remove from the fridge and cut into ¼ inch thick rounds. If not quite firm enough, you can either place it back into the fridge or roll the dough out on a surface and use a cookie cutter instead. Add the shortbread to a baking tray and bake for about 20 minutes or until golden. Remove from the oven to wire rack to cool and serve.

Ginger Shortbread

These are beautiful as they are, I think however I have friends who love adding in another ½ cup of dark chocolate chips as well.

Ingredients

2 cups all purpose flour

1 cup butter, unsalted

½ cup sugar, brown

¼ teaspoon salt

1 teaspoon vanilla

2 teaspoons ginger, ground

½ cup chopped crystallized ginger, chopped

Instructions

Preheat oven to 350F. Preheat oven. Add the butter, vanilla and sugar into a bowl and beat together until fluffy. Sift in the flour, salt and ground ginger into a separate bowl. Gradually add the flour bowl to the butter bowl, continuing to mix together as you do so. Fold in the crystallized ginger.

Make two log shapes from the dough and cover in plastic wrap. Add to the fridge for at least an hour. Remove and cut the logs so each cookie is about ¼ inch thick. Place on the baking sheet and bake for about 15 minutes or until golden. Remove and add to a wire tray to cool. Sprinkle with a little sugar before serving.

Hazelnut Shortbread

These are perfect for the Christmas season and go well with any hot drink or even a cold glass of milk.

Ingredients

2 cups all purpose flour

1 cup butter

1 cup hazelnuts, chopped

¾ cup sugar

1 teaspoon vanilla

Powdered sugar for sprinkling on top

Instructions

Preheat oven to 350F. Add the butter, vanilla and sugar into a bowl and mix until fluffy. Add in the flour and beat again and follow with the chopped hazelnuts. Fashion the dough into two evenly sized logs, cover in plastic wrap and add to the fridge for at least an hour.

Remove from the fridge and cut into ¼ inch rounds. Add to a pre-prepared baking tray and bake for about 15 minutes or until golden. Remove to a wire rack to cool. Sprinkle with a little powdered sugar and serve.

Honeyed Shortbread

Ingredients

2 cups all purpose flour

1 cup butter

½ cup honey

1 teaspoon vanilla

½ teaspoon salt

½ teaspoon cinnamon

Instructions

Preheat oven to 350F. Add the sugar, vanilla, cinnamon, honey and flour together and mix well. Sift the flour and salt into another bowl and gradually add to the butter bowl while mixing. Fashion the dough into 2 even log shapes, cover in plastic wrap and add to the fridge for at least an hour.

Remove from the fridge and cut into ¼ inch rounds. Place on a baking tray and add to the oven for about 12 minutes or until golden. Remove from the oven and place on a wire rack to cool and serve.

Jammy Shortbread Squares

These can be made with just about any variety of jam you or the family likes. Experiment with a few to decide on the favorite!

Ingredients

2 cups all purpose flour

1 cup butter

½ cup sugar

1 teaspoon vanilla

½ teaspoon salt

1 egg

1 cup jam (your choice)

Instructions

Preheat oven to 350F. Add the sugar, butter, egg and vanilla together and mix until fluffy. Add in the flour and salt and continue to mix until everything is just holding together. Add around ¾ of the dough into the pre-prepared square pan (9x9 would be ideal) and push down on the dough so it compacts. Spread your jam of choice over this layer and then add the rest of the dough over the top, crumbling it with your hand as you do so.

Bake in the oven for about 30-35 minutes or until it turns golden. Remove from the oven and leave in the pan for about 5 minutes. Remove to a wire rack to cool and cut into square shapes to serve.

Kourabiedes – Greek Shortbread

These are a staple of any Greek family or Greek celebration. They are rich and buttery. It's hard to eat more than a couple in one go but I try my best every time they're made. This will disappear before your very eyes so be quick to grab one.

There are a few elements you can change here due to supplies or personal tastes. You can use the classic Greek liquor ouzo or a brandy or a whisky if you prefer. I've gone for almonds for this recipe, but most nuts will work just as well. Pistachios is another option if you prefer.

Ingredients

3 cups all purpose flour

1 ½ cups butter

1 cups sugar, confectioners'

1 teaspoon baking powder

1 teaspoon vanilla

½ teaspoon salt

1 cup almonds, chopped

1 tablespoon brandy, ouzo or whisky

1 egg yolk

2 cups confectioners' sugar used for covering the cookies

Instructions

Preheat oven to 350F. Beat the butter and the sugar together until fluffy and add in whichever liquor you have chosen, the vanilla and the egg yolk. Follow with the flour and salt and mix until just combined. Fold in the chopped almonds.

Add a tablespoon of dough to a baking sheet. The classic shape for these cookies is a crescent-moon so fashion the dough accordingly (you can just leave them as a circle!). Add to the oven and bake for a little over 15 minutes.

Remove from the oven to a wire rack to cool for 5 minutes. Add all the confectioners' sugar into a bowl and add each cookie into it. Ensure it has a very liberal helping of sugar – it should be fully coated and white everywhere. Let them cool further on the wire rack before serving.

Lavender Shortbread

These have a charmingly delicate flavor that always seems perfect for an afternoon treat and a cup of tea. I find a couple of tablespoons of lavender flowers is fine, however you can always add a little more for a stronger impact if you prefer. I've recommended fresh however lavender can sometimes be tricky to get hold of so just go for the dried variety if required.

Ingredients

2 cups all purpose flour

1 cup butter, unsalted

½ cup sugar

½ cup confectioners' sugar

¼ teaspoon salt

2 tablespoons fresh lavender flowers, chopped

½ teaspoon vanilla

1 tablespoon lemon juice

Instructions

Preheat oven to 350F. Add the butter, vanilla, lemon juice and sugar together into a bowl and mix together until fluffy. Add in the lavender. Sift in the flour and salt into a bowl and gradually add to the butter bowl, continuing to mix as you do so. Make two log shapes from the dough, cover in plastic wrap and add to the fridge for an hour.

Once removed, cut the log shapes into rounds giving you biscuits about ¼ inch thick. Add them to a baking tray and bake for about 15 minutes or until golden. Remove to cool on a wire rack and serve.

Lemon and Thyme Shortbread

This will go nicely with a cup of tea as the thyme shines through and goes perfectly with the lemon.

Ingredients

2 cups all purpose flour

1 cup butter

½ cup sugar

½ teaspoon salt

2 tablespoons lemon zest

Juice from 1 lemon

2 tablespoons thyme

Instructions

Preheat oven to 350F. Add the butter, lemon zest and sugar together and mix until fluffy. Add the flour, salt and thyme and the lemon juice gradually until everything has just combined. Separate the dough into two even sized logs and cover in plastic wrap. Add to the fridge for an hour.

Remove and cut into ¼ inch rounds. Add to the baking sheet and bake for about 15 minutes or until golden brown. Remove to a wire rack to cool and serve.

Lemon Shortbread

I love the subtlety of the lemon coming through with the buttery shortbread here. I've opted for 4 lemons but have used as many as 8 before if I had a lot lying around for a real lemon zing taste to them.

Ingredients

2 cups all purpose flour

1 cup butter, unsalted

½ cup sugar

½ teaspoon salt

½ teaspoon vanilla

Zest of 4 lemons

Instructions

Preheat oven to 350F. Add the flour and salt to a bowl and set aside. Add the sugar and butter to another bow and beat together. Add in the vanilla and lemon zest before mixing again. Gradually add the flour mixture to the butter mixture until just combined.

Cover the dough in plastic wrap and add to the fridge for an hour. Once chilled, remove from the fridge and flatten the dough with a rolling pin to about ¼ inch thickness. Cut out in circle shape to a size of your choosing and add to a pre-prepared baking tray. Cook for about 15 minutes or until golden brown. Remove from the oven to a wire rack and allow to cool before serving.

Maple and Bacon Shortbread

I find these sweet enough already but if you want to go truly indulgent you can add ½ cup of chocolate chips as well to the recipe. This will always prove a popular breakfast treat!

Ingredients

8 bacon strips, cooked and then crumbled

1 cup butter, unsalted

½ cup maple syrup

2 tablespoons corn starch

½ cup sugar

2 cups flour

½ cup butter

Instructions

Preheat oven to 350F. Add the butter, sugar and maple syrup to a bowl and mix until fluffy. Add in the flour and the corn starch and mix until combined. Fold in the bacon. Divide the dough into two log shapes, cover in plastic wrap and add to the fridge for at least an hour.

Remove from the fridge and cut into ¼ inch thick rounds. Add the rounds to a baking sheet and bake for about 15 minutes or until golden. Remove from the oven to a wire rack to cool and serve.

Matcha and Chocolate Shortbread

These are simple to make but are a great combination and look stunning with the chocolate coating. I tend to go for milk chocolate, but they look amazing with white chocolate as well – or go for the combination!

Ingredients

2 cups all purpose flour

1 cup butter

½ cup sugar

1 teaspoon vanilla

½ teaspoon salt

2 tablespoons Match powder

Frosting

1 cup mini chocolate chips

Instructions

Preheat oven to 350F. Add the butter, vanilla and sugar into a bowl and mix until fluffy. Add in the flour, matcha powder and salt until everything has just come together. Remove the dough and shape into a ball. Cover with plastic wrap and add to the fridge for an hour.

Remove from the fridge and place on a floured surface. Roll out the dough to about ¼ inch thickness and cut with a cookie cutter. Add the shortbread to a baking tray and bake for about 15 minutes. Remove to a wire rack to cool.

Melt the chocolate chips in the microwave or in a glass bowl over boiling water. Take each cooled biscuit and dip half into the melted chocolate. Return to the wire rack for the chocolate to harden and serve.

Millionaire's Shortbread

This beautiful combination of shortbread, caramel and chocolate is a classic that proves itself a hit over and over again. It takes a little longer in preparation than some recipes but the beautiful sheen of the chocolate on top and the sweet caramel hidden underneath makes it all worthwhile.

Ingredients

2 cups all purpose flour

1 cup butter

½ cup sugar

1 teaspoon vanilla

½ cup sugar

½ teaspoon salt

Caramel

1 cup butter

1/3 cup sugar, brown

1 cup chocolate chips, semi-sweet

1 14 oz can condensed milk

Chocolate Topping

1 cup chocolate chips, dark

Sea salt

Instructions

Preheat oven to 350F. Start with the base by adding the butter, sugar and vanilla together and beating until fluffy. Add in the flour and salt until everything is just combined with over-beating. Add the dough to a pre-prepared 9x9 pan and push down firmly so it compacts well. Add to the oven and bake for about 20 minutes until golden. Remove from the oven and cool.

Now start on the caramel by adding the sugar, condensed milk and butter into a saucepan over low to medium heat. Carry on stirring until the butter has fully melted and the contents of the pan start to boil. Turn the heat down to a simmer and carry on stirring. In a few minutes it will thicken and turn caramel color. Now pour over the pan. Smooth out with a knife and add to the fridge for at least an hour.

Make the topping by melting the chocolate chips in a microwave or a glass bowl over water. Let it cool for 10 minutes and then pour over the caramel. Sprinkle just a little sea salt over the chocolate and add back to the fridge for a couple of hours before serving.

Mocha Shortbread

Coffee and chocolate is always a good combination and these are no exceptions. Try it with the white chocolate glaze for a little extra sweet touch!

Ingredients

2 cups all purpose flour

½ cup butter

½ cup sugar

1/3 cup cocoa powder

1 teaspoon vanilla

½ teaspoon salt

2 teaspoons instant coffee granules

Optional Glaze

½ cup white chocolate chips

Instructions

Preheat oven to 350F. Add the sugar, vanilla and butter to a bowl and beat until fluffy. Add the cocoa powder, coffee, flour and salt and mix until combined. Add a full teaspoon of the dough onto the prepared baking sheet. Bake for 12 minutes or until golden and remove to a wire rack to cool.

Heat the white chocolate chips in a glass bowl over boiling water carefully. Drizzle over the biscuits, let the chocolate set and serve with a cup of steaming coffee!

Nutella Shortbread

What's better than a Nutella recipe? A Nutella recipe with chocolate chips of course!

Ingredients

2 cups all purpose flour

½ cup butter

½ cup sugar

½ cup Nutella

1 teaspoon vanilla

1 cup chocolate chips

Instructions

Preheat oven to 350F. Add the butter, vanilla and sugar together and beat until fluffy. Add in the Nutella and beat again. Now add the flour, mix again and fold in the chocolate chips. Divide the dough into two evenly sized log shapes and cover in plastic wrap. Add to the fridge for at least an hour.

Remove and cut into rounds that are roughly ¼ inch think. If it's not quite firm enough, then roll out the dough and cut into squares or use a cookie cutter of your preferred size to make the cuts. Add to a baking sheet and bake for around 15-17 minutes. Remove from the oven to cool on a wire rack and serve.

Oatmeal Shortbread

Oats are perfect in many Scottish dishes and they work equally well in shortbread as well. They add a slightly different texture to a more traditional shortbread recipe and are also exceptionally easy to create.

Ingredients

2 cups all purpose flour

1 ½ cups butter, unsalted

1 teaspoon salt

2 cups oats, rolled

1 ½ cups sugar

Confectioners' sugar for decoration

Instructions

Preheat oven to 350F. Add the butter and sugar into a bowl and mix together until creamy. Add the oats, salt and flour and mix again. Fashion the dough into two log shapes, cover in plastic wrap and add to the fridge for an hour. Once chilled, remove from the fridge and cut rounds to about ¼ inch thickness. Add the biscuits to a baking tray.

Bake for about 30 minutes or until golden. Remove to a wire rack to cool before serving. Top with sugar and serve.

Orange Shortbread

Ingredients

2 cups all purpose flour

1 cup butter, unsalted

½ cup sugar

2 tablespoons orange zest

1 teaspoon vanilla

½ teaspoon salt

1 cup chocolate chips

Instructions

Preheat the oven to 350F. Add the flour and salt into a bowl and set to one side. Add the butter and sugar to another bowl and cream together. Add in the vanilla and orange zest and mix again. Gradually add the contents of the flour bowl into the butter bowl continuing to mix it in.

Remove the dough from the bowl and fashion it into a log shape. Wrap in plastic film and add to the fridge for at least an hour. Once chilled, remove and cut into slices about ¼ inch wide. Add the slices onto a baking sheet and bake for about 15 minutes or until browned. Remove from the oven and add to a wire rack.

Melt the choc chips in a microwave or in a bowl over boiling water. Drizzle the melted chocolate over the shortbread and serve.

Peach Shortbread

Ingredients

2 cups all purpose flour

1 cup butter

½ cup sugar

1 teaspoon vanilla

½ teaspoon cinnamon

½ teaspoon salt

3 peaches sliced

1 egg

Instructions

Preheat oven to 350F. Add the sugar, flour, cinnamon and salt into a bowl and whisk together. Add in the butter, followed by the egg and continue to mix until you everything just starts to hold together. Add a little over ¾ of the dough into a pre-prepared baking pan and press down lightly so the mixture compacts. Now add the thinly sliced peaches over the top. Add the rest of the mixture to the top of the peaches and press down very lightly again.

Add to the oven for about 30 minutes. Remove from the oven and give it 5 minutes to cool in the pan. Place on a wire rack to cool and then cut it into squares. You can serve warm with some extra peaches and ice-cream on the side or have them just as they are!

Peanut Butter Choc Chip Shortbread

The delicious creamy flavour and texture of the peanut butter shines through with these cookies, strongly enhanced with the addition of the chocolate chips. I have tried this with white chocolate chips before which works well although my preferred option is milk. You will have to make them a few times to decide on your personal favorite!

Ingredients

2 cups all purpose flour

½ cup butter

½ cup peanut butter

½ cup sugar, brown

½ teaspoon salt

1 teaspoon vanilla

1 cup mini choc chips

Instructions

Preheat oven to 350F. Add the butter, peanut butter, sugar and vanilla into a bowl and mix together. Add the flour and salt into the bowl gradually and mix again. Fold in the chocolate chips. Remove the dough and divide into 2 equal sized logs. Cover in plastic wrap and add to the fridge for at least an hour.

Remove from the fridge and cut into rounds, roughly ¼ inch thick. Add the rounds to a baking sheet and bake for about 12 minutes or until golden. Remove from the heat and place on a wire rack to cool and serve.

Peppermint and Chocolate Shortbread

Ingredients

2 cups all purpose flour

1 cup butter, unsalted

½ teaspoon salt

½ cup sugar, powdered

1 teaspoon vanilla

1 cup peppermint chips or crushed peppermint candies

½ cup chocolate chips

Instructions

Preheat oven to 350F. Add the butter, vanilla and sugar together and beat until fluffy. Gradually add the flour and salt and mix until just combined. Fold in the peppermints and the chocolate chips into the mixture. Divide the dough into two equal logs, cover in plastic wrap and add to the fridge for at least an hour.

Remove and cut the log shapes into ¼ inch rounds. Add to a baking tray and bake for 15 minutes or until golden. Remove and place on a wire rack to cool. Sprinkle with a dusting of sugar and serve.

Pineapple Shortbread

These are a great spring treat and always seem to herald the arrival of warmer weather for me. You can make them during the colder months though for a festive feel!

Ingredients

2 cup all purpose flour

1 cup butter

½ cup sugar

1 teaspoon vanilla

½ teaspoon salt

¾ cup dried pineapple

Frosting

8 ounces cream cheese

½ cup confectioners' sugar

1 teaspoon pineapple juice or water

¼ cup dried pineapple

Instructions

Preheat oven to 350F. Add the butter, vanilla and sugar together and beat together until fluffy. Add in the flour and salt until just combined. Fold in the dried pineapple. Remove the dough and separate into two equal sized logs. Cover in plastic wrap and add to the fridge for at least an hour.

Remove from the fridge and cut into ¼ inch thick rounds. Add to a pre-prepared baking tray and bake for 12-14 minutes or golden. Remove to a wire rack and allow to cool.

Prepare the frosting by combining the cream cheese and sugar. If it's a little thick, you can add some more liquid. If too runny, add a little more sugar. Once the desired consistency is reached, spoon a little frosting on each cookie and garnish with the remaining pineapple pieces. Allow everything to set and serve.

Pistachio and Chocolate Shortbread

Ingredients

2 cups all purpose flour

1 cup butter

½ cup sugar

½ teaspoon salt

1 cup pistachios, chopped

1 teaspoon vanilla

1 cup chocolate chips

Instructions

Preheat oven to 350F. Add the butter, vanilla and sugar together and mix until fluffy. Add the flour and salt and mix again. Fold in the pistachios. Cover the dough with plastic wrap and add to the fridge for an hour. Then remove and roll out the dough so it is roughly ¼ inch thick. Use a cookie cutter to cut your cookies into shape and add to a baking tray. Bake for about 13-14 minutes or until golden.

Remove from the oven to a wire rack to cool. Melt your chocolate chips in the microwave or in a glass bowl over boiling water. Dip one half of the cookie into the melted chocolate and return to the wire rack to set. You can add a few large sea salt flakes as a final touch or serve as they are.

Poppy Seed Shortbread

Ingredients

2 cups all purpose flour

1 cup butter

½ cup sugar

½ teaspoon salt

2 teaspoons vanilla

2 tablespoons poppy seeds

Instructions

Preheat oven to 350F and add parchment paper to a 9 x 13 inch pan. Add the butter, vanilla and sugar into a bowl and mix together until fluffy. Add the flour, salt and poppy seeds and mix again until everything has just combined. Add all the mixture to the pan, cover in plastic wrap and add to the fridge for at least an hour.

Add to the oven and bake for 30 minutes or until golden. Remove from the oven to a wire rack and cut into squares or a rectangular shape if you prefer. Let them cool and then serve.

Pumpkin Chocolate Drizzled Shortbread

These make a great autumnal treat – try dishing them out for Halloween rather than candy for a change that will be loved by all who try them!

Ingredients

2 cups all purpose flour

½ cup butter

½ cup sugar, brown

½ teaspoon salt

½ cup pumpkin puree

1 teaspoon cinnamon

½ teaspoon vanilla

1 teaspoon pumpkin pie spice

1 cup mini choc chips

Instructions

Preheat oven to 350F. Add the butter, sugar and vanilla to a bowl and mix together until fluffy. Add in the flour, salt, cinnamon and pumpkin pie spice and mix again. Having extracted as much moisture as possible from the pumpkin puree, add it to the dough and mix again. Prepare an 8x8 inch baking tray and add the dough evenly around. Bake for around 40 minutes or until it is golden brown. Remove from the oven and place on a wire rack to cool. Cut into squares once cooled

Melt the chocolate chips in the microwave or in a glass bowl over boiling water. Gently drizzle the top of the squares with the melted chocolate and serve.

Raisin and Orange Shortbread

Ingredients

2 cups all purpose flour

1 cup butter, unsalted

½ teaspoon salt

½ cup sugar

1 teaspoon vanilla

1 cup raisins

Zest from two oranges

Instructions

Preheat oven to 350F. Add the sugar, vanilla and butter together and mix until fluffy. Add in the flour and salt and mix. Fold in the raisins and orange zest. Divide the mixture into two equal sized log shapes and cover in plastic wrap. Add to the fridge for at least an hour.

Remove from the fridge and cut into ¼ inch thick rounds. Place the rounds on a baking sheet and bake for about 15 minutes or until just golden brown. Remove to a wire rack to cool and then serve.

Rhubarb Shortbread Slices

Ingredients

2 cups all purpose flour

1 cup butter

½ cup sugar

1 teaspoon vanilla

½ teaspoon salt

Filling

2 cups rhubarb, chopped

1/3 cup water

½ cup sugar

Instructions

Preheat oven to 350F. Add the butter, vanilla and sugar together and mix until fluffy. Add the flour and salt and mix again until just combined. Cover the dough in plastic wrap and add to the fridge for an hour.

Make the filling by adding the rhubarb, sugar and the water into a pan and gently cooking for about 15 minutes until the rhubarb softens. Remove the pan from the heat to cool.

Remove the dough from the fridge and add 2/3 of it into a pre-prepared 9x13 inch pan. Press lightly down on the dough. Spread the cooled rhubarb all over the tin. Add the remaining 1/3 of dough on top of the rhubarb. Add to the oven and bake for about 30-35 minutes or until golden.

Allow the shortbread to cool on a wire rack and cut into squares to serve alone or warm with cream or vanilla ice-cream.

S 'Mores Shortbread

Everything gets better with chocolate and marshmallows. It gets better still with the addition of shortbread. Try these for a popular, sweet treat.

Ingredients

2 cups all purpose flour

1 cup butter

½ cup sugar

1 teaspoon salt

1 cup graham crackers, crumbled

1 cup mini chocolate chips

1 cup mini marshmallows

Instructions

Preheat oven to 350F. Add the butter and sugar together and mix well. Gradually add in the flour, graham crackers and salt and mix again. Fashion the dough into two log shapes, cover in plastic wrap and add to the fridge for at least an hour. Remove from the fridge and cut into ¼ inch thick rounds.

Add the rounds to a baking tray and bake for about 15 minutes or until golden. While cooking, melt the chocolate chips in the microwave or in a glass bowl over boiling water. Remove the cookies from the oven and place on a wire rack to cool. Once cooled, add the chocolate to the shortbread and 2 or 3 mini marshmallows to each shortbread before serving.

Vanilla and Chai Shortbread

These have a lovely spicy taste to them and of course go beautifully with a cup of tea. Popular at Christmas time of course but I enjoy having them throughout the year.

Ingredients

2 cups all purpose flour

1 cup butter, unsalted

½ teaspoon salt

½ cup sugar

1 teaspoon vanilla

1 black tea teabag

1 teaspoon cardamom

1 teaspoon cinnamon

½ teaspoon nutmeg

½ teaspoon ground cloves

Instructions

Preheat oven to 350F. Add the cardamom, cinnamon, nutmeg, cloves and contents of the teabag together and mix well before setting aside. In a separate bowl, add the butter, vanilla and sugar and mix until just combined. Add in the flour and salt and mix until just combined. Separate the dough into two even log shapes, cover in plastic wrap and add to the fridge for at least an hour.

Once removed, cut into ¼ inch rounds. Bake for about 20 minutes or until golden. Remove to a wire rack to cool and serve with tea.

Vanilla Rose Shortbread

As much as I love a rich chocolate shortbread, sometimes a more delicate and lighter flavour is all I need These shortbread cookies are perfect for that time.

I always have these with a cup of tea in the afternoon. A few minutes of quiet, reflective bliss in a busy day is just perfect.

Ingredients

2 cup all purpose flour

1 cup butter

½ cup sugar

1 teaspoon vanilla

1 teaspoon rosewater

½ teaspoon salt

1 tablespoon edible rose petals, crushed

Instructions

Preheat oven to 350F. Add the butter, vanilla and sugar together and mix until fluffy. Add in the flour, salt and rose petals and mix until everything is just combined.

Gradually add in the teaspoon of rosewater (you can always add a little more if you prefer a stronger rosewater tint of course).

Separate the dough into two evenly sized log shapes and cover with plastic wrap. Add to the fridge for at least an hour.

Remove from the fridge and roll onto a floured surface to about ¼ inch thickness. Bake for 12-14 minutes or until just golden. Remove from the oven, place on a wire rack to cool and serve with tea.

White Chocolate Shortbread

These look wonderful with extra decorations of your own choosing on top. They always seem a rather Christmas-like treat to me with the white chocolate on the top being the snow, but they taste great at any time of the year.

Ingredients

2 cups all purpose flour

½ cup butter

½ cup sugar

1 teaspoon vanilla

½ teaspoon salt

1 cup white chocolate chips

Glitter or any decoration topping of your choice

Instructions

Preheat oven to 350F. Add the butter, vanilla and sugar to a bowl and mix until fluffy. Add in the salt and flour and mix. Fold in half a cup of the white chocolate chips. Take a heaped teaspoon of dough and place it on a prepared baking sheet. Press the dough down lightly with the back of the spoon so it becomes flattened. Bake for about 12 minutes or until golden and remove to a wire rack to cool.

Melt the remainder of the white chocolate chips using a double boiler or a glass bowl over boiling water. Take each cookie and dip the top of the cookie into the melted chocolate. Return to the wire rack and then add in whatever decoration you like. Let the chocolate set hard and serve.

Made in the USA
San Bernardino, CA
16 November 2019